Central Heating

poems about fire and warmth

by **Marilyn Singer**

illustrated by **Meilo So**

Alfred A. Knopf
New York

To Janet Schulman, who provided the spark.

And with thanks to Steve Aronson, Kelly Milner Halls,
and all my other friends whose poetic advice I value,
and to everyone at Knopf/Random House for their support.
—Marilyn Singer

THIS IS A BORZOI BOOK PUBLISHED BY ALFRED A. KNOPF

Text copyright © 2005 by Marilyn Singer
Illustrations copyright © 2005 by Meilo So

www.randomhouse.com/kids

Library of Congress Cataloging-in-Publication Data
Singer, Marilyn.
Central heating : poems about fire and warmth / Marilyn Singer ;
illustrated by Meilo So — 1st ed.
p. cm.
ISBN 0-375-82912-1 (trade) — ISBN 0-375-92912-6 (lib. bdg.)
1. Fire—Juvenile poetry. 2. Heat—Juvenile poetry. 3. Children's poetry,
American. I. So, Meilo, ill. II. Title.
PS3569.I546C46 2005
811'.54—dc22
2004004274

MANUFACTURED IN MALAYSIA

January 2005

10   9   8   7   6   5   4   3   2   1

First Edition

Contents

Contradiction

Fire has contradiction
      at its heart,
from that wintry blue part
      to its jagged golden crown.
It gives comfort
      in a candle's cozy flickering.
It brings terror
      in a forest's burning down.
It is both the bolt of lightning
      that splits a summer sky
and the burst of July fireworks
      that unites a wide-eyed town.
From its smoldering end
      to its sudden start,
Fire has contradiction
      at its heart.

Fire-Bringers

It must have been some job,
> that task of carrying
>> precious fire
> from Stone Age camp to camp.
Holding high a flaming branch
> like an Olympic torch,
or bearing embers in a coconut husk,
> a pink-edged shell.
Taking care it never went out.
Was it the finest athlete,
> the wisest mother, the oldest granddad
>> who had the honor?
How many children dreamed
> of following in their footsteps?
Could any have imagined
> metal pots and matches,
> chimneys and tinderboxes,
>> and kitchens with cheerful potbellied stoves?

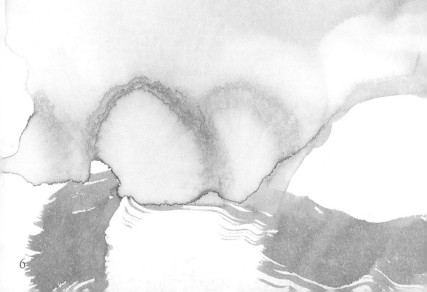

Appetite

Fire is always hungry.

    Meat or fish

    Carrots or eggplant

    Math books, French tests

    Overstuffed sofas, junkyard automobiles

    Tenements, castles

    A stylish café, an old-fashioned street—

Some treats it gobbles,

    Others it savors slowly

        leaving a few stones, a bunch of bricks.

Fire is the least fussy of diners.

It likes almost anything

    it licks.

Landmark

The old house next door
    sat boring, ignored
until the fire came
    and threw a peculiar party.
Neighbors in hats and coats
    gathered on the sidewalk, spilled into the street,
gawking, talking to folks they'd never greeted before,
watching flames light up windows too long dark,
listening to the loud music of sirens, cell phones, radios,
cheering the firemen in shiny striped coats
    spraying water like silver holiday streamers.

The old house next door
    sits charred, empty,
a landmark for citizens, street historians,
    would-be buyers,
and brand-new tenants: squirrels and pigeons,
    carrying acorns into the boarded-up basement,
    laying eggs on the blackened windowsills.

Forged

To understand metal,
    make friends with fire,
get to know its quirks,
    how it works,
if you want to forge a shovel, a horseshoe,
    a band of gold.
To understand fire,
get to know wood,
      coal, gas, peat, oil,
    how it feeds,
      what it needs to melt iron, copper, bronze,
      to bring silver to a boil.
Learn the rules of air's games
    at fanning flames.
Leave yourself no room for doubt.
To understand metal,
      make friends with fire—
      how to ignite it,
      how to put it out.

Fire Fighters

Wailing and pulsing, the rig
      rips down the street.
Inside, truckies and pumper crew,
      turned out in their own kind of armor,
        ride,
ready with crowbars and axes,
a thousand gallons of water, a hundred yards of hose
      to knock down the angry Orange Man.
In the heat of battle,
they don't think about winning
      till they've already won.

15

Dragon

Who wouldn't care to be
      a dragon?
To be master of fire
      and air?
To wander through a field or two
      torching ricks of hay?
To take to the sky and declare you're there
      with a fireworks display?
In winter not to worry if it's snowing
      or it's sleeting?
To snuggle in a pleasant cave
      where you're the central heating?

Hot Water

Of all the creatures craving heat,
we're the fauna
      that like a sauna
      a sweat lodge, hot tub
      Turkish bath, or shower
to warm us up
to clean us off
to make us perspire
to give us time to contemplate
      water, steam, and fire.

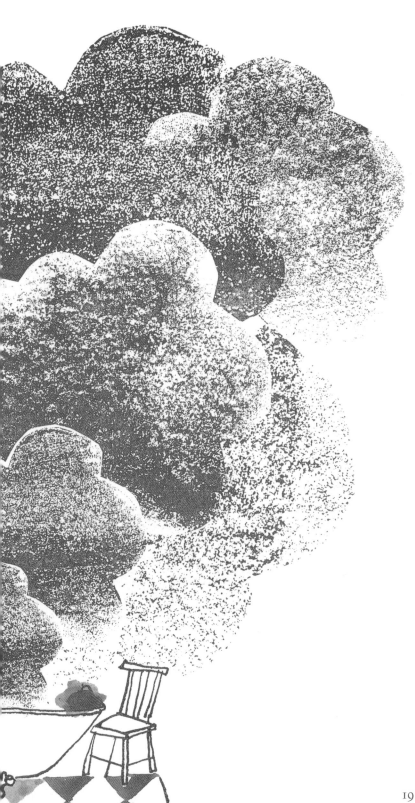

Chili Peppers

A pitcher of water,
A bucket of ice,
A bathtub of grape juice—
Will nothing suffice
      to put out the fire
           from one bit of spice?
The hot jalapeño that hid in my rice!

Birthday Party

Blow them out!
Mom says the guests are all waiting
        for dessert.
But I want to watch them burn,
        to give each little flame
                its full glory.
To see what happens then
        to the white frosting
                and pink roses.
To make my birthday stretch
        beyond the ordinary
        into the memorable:
the time I let the candles
        take the cake.

Toasting Marshmallows

It hinges on a second, an inch.
A shade too long, a hair too close,
    and perfect crisp brown
        turns to bitter charcoal,
    gentle melting
        becomes ooze.
And you lose the game,
      the marshmallow
        to the flame.

Distance from the Sun

Looking at the solar system
     hanging from the ceiling of my room,
those miniature spheres forever fixed
     so near or so far
          from that garish orange star,
I think of bowls of porridge,
     most too hot or cold,
but one, amazingly, just right.
On behalf of Goldilocks, three bears,
     and one blue planet,
I tip my hat to the ongoing miracle
     of perfect
        placement.

Center of the Earth

No matter how snowy the Wyoming plains
> how icy the Iceland hills
> how chilly the Atlantic waters

No matter how frigid the spot,
> it sits atop a bubbling cauldron of molten rock
> that finds a way to shoot up
>> streams of glowing lava, jets of steamy water,
>> fountains of sky-high fire, bursts of boiling mud,
> reminding us that the earth's deep pot
>> is always cooking
>> always hot.

Desert Day

Denizens of the desert
        understand under, inside,
        between, below.
Each rattlesnake, wren,
        rabbit, fox, or spider
lays claim to every scrubby tree and cactus,
        arroyo, burrow, boulder, branch
to sleep, or sit out the sun.
And when moving is a must,
        they wheel, flap, sidewind, scuttle,
        run across the blistering sand.
Denizens of the desert
        learn to balance
        the stillness and the scramble.
Few amble.

Prairie Fire

Shaggy and calm
  as the distant grassy hills,
the bison stop to graze
  at the edge of the burning plain.
Not for them the lost songs
  of nest, egg, tree, home.
Fearless as fire,
  swifter than flames,
like their cousins, the elk, the deer,
they travel to their own ancient tune:
Mother, Father,
  we have seen this before.
Daughter, Son,
  we will see this again.

33

Forest Fire

Fire silences the choir
    darkens the room
    empties the hall
    opens the door
for the hawks, coyotes, and flycatchers
    waiting to greet the fleeing mice, rabbits,
    and gnats;
for the woodpeckers
cleaning the ruined trees of burrowing beetles;
for the bright pink fireweed, rare lilies,
    and lodgepole pines,
skilled decorators who will roll out a carpet
    for the visitors and performers to come,
      bringing new music
      singing new songs.

Summer Magic

Any night in June
I can become a wizard
    carrying in my warm hands
        a cool flashing glow
            the color of topaz or peridot.
Such a surprising light
    without sparks, without heat—
        a remarkable feat.
Real magic conjured from the dusky summer sky
    (with the aid of my assistant,
        Firefly).

Holidays

Holidays are marked by fire:
Sparklers in summer,
Jack-o'-lanterns in fall.
Menorahs, luminarias,
Christmas lights mimicking flames
     of yuletides past.
Paper lanterns afloat
     in Japanese harbors,
          sending departed spirits on their way.
Clay lamps shining
     in Indian streets,
          greeting goddesses and each new year.
So much light and warmth,
So much hope reflected
     in watchful eyes,
          joyous or solemn,
          pale or dark,
All year long in our brilliant worldwide
     gala.

Inspiration

No bomb
No bazooka
No dynamite
No baked potato
No tea for two
No barbecue
No cigarette
No incense
No smoke signals
No phone
No electric guitar
No TV star
No chandelier
No streetlight
No candle in the dark
No tension
No invention—
    without a spark.

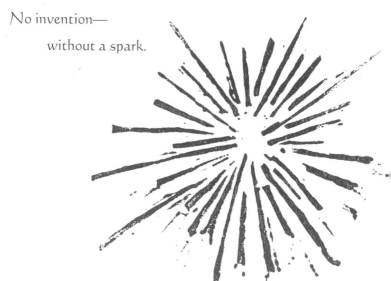